Perceptions of a Blue Lotus

A collection of poems depicting perceptions on life and matters that matter

Heena Bhatia

BookLeaf Publishing
India | USA | UK

Made with ❤ on the BookLeaf Publishing Platform
www.bookleafpub.in
www.bookleafpub.com

Dedication

This book of poems is dedicated to all those people who have loved and lost, who have fallen and stood up after each fall, who have been burned and who resurrected from the ashes, and to all you deep thinkers. This book is also dedicated to those who are struggling to find their faith and inner fire. You are seen, you are blessed, and you are not alone in this journey.

Acknowledgment

This book is a result of my experiences, epiphanies, observations, and the treasure trove of firsthand experience of the knowledge, faith, and grit I have seen and felt in the world around and within me. These poems are a reflection of my deepest thoughts and feelings and experiences of blessings. Inspired by the men, women, and children, I have witnessed throughout my life till now, this book reflects the paradox of the complexity but simplicity of life and all that makes up life.

The most important force behind this book is the blessings of Sadhguru that found me when I was at my lowest, pulled me up, and filled me with so much grace and life that I found the words to write this book.

Preface

Dear Reader,

The spirit of life is indomitable—it experiences a series of pain and happiness throughout life, but somehow the pain stays with us for longer, as it is the deepest emotion most of us feel. Happiness tries hard to stay with us, but we choose to surpass those moments as we are constantly looking for ways to grow, and pain brings growth—but does it? Pain brings with it tremendous lessons and forces us to look deeper within ourselves and find the light that keeps us going despite all odds. This is where happiness meets us again. Pain and happiness are the two sides of the same coin—always co-existing. Have you ever thought about what would it be if we chose to always retain our happiness and growth, with or without going through pain—for that we would need to see them with a different lens of life.

Life as we know it is full of possibilities, yet we carry the ghosts of our past, present, and future constantly on our backs, thus taking away the joy of life from ourselves and losing our authentic selves. The joy with which we navigate it all and the way we live our lives depend on the way we perceive all that is happening around us. Our perceptions become our reality, and the poems in this book reflect a different or a clearer perception toward life with the intent that it helps you find joy—joy of acceptance, joy of surrender, or even joy of knowing you are not alone.

An ever-evolving state of being is the only constant, yet we stagnate ourselves with limiting beliefs. So if you are prepared to delve into a world of a new perception of life and things around you, this book is for you.

Answers

She looked at the morning sky
Wondering who had the answers to pacify her mind
A mind fluttering with fear
And questions
A heart palpitating anxiously
With a fear of tomorrow
And a regret of yesterday

She looked at the passing stream
Wondering who had the answers to pacify her
inner voice
A voice that was quiet on the outside
A voice that was screaming to be set free
A voice that was sure of what it wanted
A voice that was waiting to be heard

She looked at the dandelion floating away
with the breeze
Wondering who had the answers to satisfy her
curious self
A self that was wondering about its purpose
A self that was questioning all existence
A self that was trying to find meaning in it all

She looked at the setting sun
Enthralled in its beauty
And for an instant, she forgot all those
questions
That moment was all that she needed
She felt gratitude for her humanity
That made her question it all
That made her feel deeply
That made her care truly

A gift that came drowned with its ignorance
But a gift that came equipped to find the
answers
There was no more rush
Only a lifetime of self-exploration to go

Inside we perceive

Being is the slave
Being is the master
Being is the winner
Being is the loser
Wanting to be nothing
Wanting to be everything

Being is the sky
Being is the earth
Being is fire
Being is the rain
Wanting to be provider
Wanting to be provided

Being is the lover
Being is the beloved
Being is the believer
Being is the atheist
Having felt nothing
Having felt everything

Being is the creator
Being is the created
Being is the destroyer
Being is the destroyed
Having given nothing
Having given everything

Being could be the incumbent
Only if it allowed its eyes to see
Being could be nothing
Being could be everything
Only inside
Only inside we perceive

Unforgettable

They wallowed in her beauty
They thronged in her fame
They decided she was the queen
Albeit without a name

She rode the tide
With each growing stride
Like a drug, it eroded her insides
The high, self-consuming
The craziness, self-absorbing
She lost her soul in exchange

Beauty wore off
And so did the novelty
She was an old flame
Destined to lose eventually

They pitied her
Then they bullied her
They were finally disgusted
In the end, they replaced her
No one chased her
In their hearts, she was ousted

She was just a pretty face
Albeit left without a trace
Another story, another farce
Of a life lived without grace
Life lost, meaninglessly
Seeking its true meaning
In something completely fake
Wishing there was something more to make

Potential

Still today, like a lifeless body
Stood a life that was pushed to always act
Floating away like a feather in the wind
Went a mind that earlier worked on
perfection

Lost in the tide of time
Stood a soul as vast as an ocean
Looking in the mirror with uneasy eyes
Stood a beauty that enchanted the world

A reflection came over
And shoved a thorn in its chest
Suddenly awake with no fear or fury
Stood a life with eyes full of determination
It smiled and stood tall
Chin up and now ready
To take up the next battle
It's real, self-revealed inside
With its being, now rejuvenated
It took an impulse and a test but
Its true self revealed itself at last

Twins

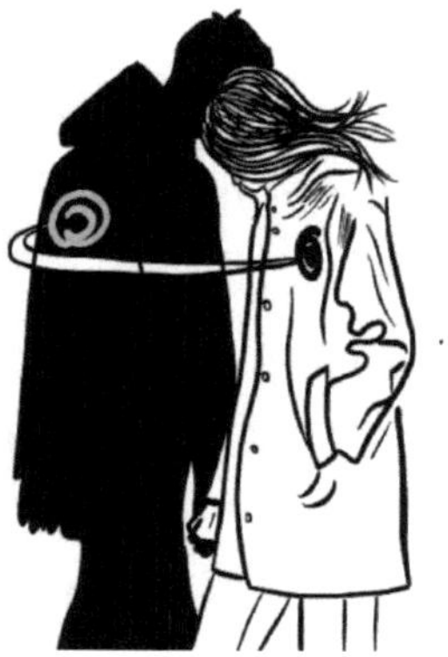

Attached and detached at the same time
Their love, they thought, stood the test of
time
Together they had flourished and grown
Now ready to climb another level

One day, one thought, I am always the one
giving
Other day, other thought, I am always the one
forgiving
Then one said to another, I am done I am
done
Ok said the other, expecting life now to be
fun

With no obligations and no boundaries
Enjoying the fruits of their labors
They thought they would be better off
No giving, no forgiving
No rules, no bonds
What they lost was symbiotic
What they threw away, profound

With time, the glory was now all gone
They remained unseen, unspoken
The twins were feeding off each other
Too arrogant and thus now broken

Transient

Overlooking the horizon
She saw the first morning sun
Gleaming in the beauty and hope
Wishes surging and faith enhancing
She prepared to run the race
Energized and exhilarated

The beauty of it faded with time
Harsh rays piercing her very being
She ran for cover
from its cruel glare
With beads of sweat running down her face
and the heat sucking out all life from her
Frail with the pain
She wanted to quit
But time reminded her
she was not done yet

Shade gave her some hope
She slowly quenched her thirst
Regaining her stride, she now rose
Taking it slowly at first
The sun now moved away
Bringing with it the glory of the sunset
The subtle light helped her soar
Gaining glory, she ran till she crossed the finish line

She enjoyed her victory
But soon came the night
It gave her a fright
Would everything she earned fade away
Soon out came the moon
Gleaming with light in her heart
She danced in its rays
Full of life and love

Soaking it all in, never wanting it to end
But sleep took over and she drifted away
Having felt pain and love
Never to rise as the race was now done
Transient was its every phase

Gathering

She huffed and puffed
Running as soon as she opened her eyes
Gathering leaves fallen off
To decorate her house of straw
To fix her crown of thorns
To show her life meant more

Spent her peak hours hoarding
Spent the remaining cleaning
Spending energy managing the thorns
Showing off her meaning to all
Loving and caring for withering willows
Spent her peak time chasing greens

The leaves soon wilted
Her energy now down
The storm blew away the straw
Finally, she dropped down spent
Now she lay entangled in the web of deceit
In the wilted leaves she owned

Gathering her dust the wind blew away
Only if she could see
The love she should have accumulated
Would have set her free

Harmony

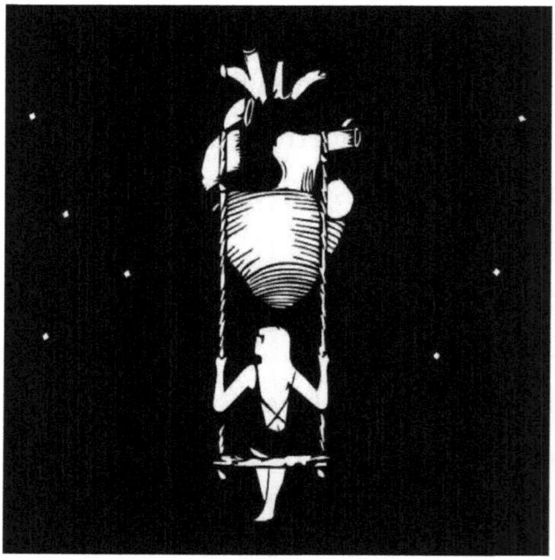

The mind spoke in a language the heart couldn't hear
The heart beat too fast, intervening in the peace of the mind

The eyes saw all the mess around
The love could not be found
The tongue lashed out critically
The ears filled with sounds
The hands thrashed
The feet crashed
Her skin scorching under the sun

Till she heard a song
A rhythm of the divine
Bringing harmony to her heartbeat
Silencing her fears
Wiping away her tears
Slowly binding together her soul
Her consciousness rose
Her life did unfold
Heart and brain now became one

Limits

Laughing out loud
Wearing clothes that she liked
Never bothered by opinions
An insatiable taste for life
She was a woman who didn't know her limit
Her light too much, her aura too bright

Leaving her home
For a man who she loved
While the world called her mad
For being with someone like him
Never bothered by looks
An undeniable love that binds
She was a woman who didn't know her limit
Her passion too much, her desire too bright

Giving it all
Asking for nothing in return
While her world now turned sad
As her love was taken for granted
Never caring for things
A heart that was now broken
She was a woman who didn't know her limit
Her pain too much, her light now dimmed

Her heart finally stopped
Last breaths now counting
While the loved ones cried
For a life that was dimmed by their pride
Her crime was that of loving, having a heart
that could not hide
She was a woman who didn't know her limit
And was now finally free
Their loss too much, her light now limitless

Conscientious

Kindness clearly apparent
Love so very abundant
Hoping to work for a better world
Wanting to be love redefined

Waiting patiently for the intellect to sing along
Creating simultaneously a wave too strong
Intellect demanded a profit sheet
Asking for outcomes and results
Focusing on the tragic
In reality, there is no magic

Kindness had no answers
Let us just do it to serve, it said
Not impressed, intellect then frowned
Grow up Grow up, it sighed
Life had too many expectations
Winning, losing many a time
Keeping up with changing times
Losing hope and time
Kindness walked out of the door
Intellect won the battle
Leaving the consciousness
away to wilt and wane

The world keeps revolving
While he plays the game of fame
Well to give him credit
He did reveal his true self in some rare
moments

Now he looks in the mirror; his eyes reek of
terror
Wondering if he made the right choice, to
give up on his consciousness forever

Too pretty, too petty

She wore the latest trends
Danced at the hottest joints
Men tried to buy her love
Women tried to get her to spill the beans
She was pretty but she wasn't for sale
She loved life but she wasn't a fail

She felt too deeply
She cared too intensely
Like a dandelion, she wanted to fly
She wanted to be timeless

Trapped in prejudices around
Her heart too strong to hear any noise
She continued to live her life strong
Unattached but caring for those who belong

Caged

Gen Z, millennial, Gen alpha
South Mumbai, Gurgaon, suburbs, tier 2 girl
They labeled her at every move
She didn't agree to be caged
She was a girl who wanted to live
She wasn't a label or role model
She was a bird, free and uncaged
Those who couldn't understand her wanted
her in a box

When she was heartbroken
What are you? They said
You are a Gen Z, just chill.
Swipe right and you will find someone new

When she cared too much about her job
What are you? They said
You are a Millennial, just chill
You will find something else to do

When she took time for her passions
They turned her balance into attitude
What are you? They said
You are Gen Alpha—of course, you don't care

When she stood up for what she deserved
They turned her rights into pride
What are you? They said
You are a South Mumbai girl; of course, you are privileged

She didn't fit in a box, nor did she want to be caged
She was a girl who wanted to live with flair
Not to be judged for being herself
Not to be labelled for her truth

The Elevator

The mother and daughter
Got into an elevator together
Each on her phone
Looking for love from hundreds of strangers

No words
No glances
No emotion
Not even a sigh

They got into the car quietly together
And into the metaverse
Looking for the words left unsaid, the
emotions uncovered

With likes, comments, and shares, they hope
to find love
The hope that was shattered
The sun that was burnt out
The galaxy that collapsed
The life that lost the battle
In the hope to find itself
In the half truth

The wrong door

That is not where I am supposed to be
Banging on the wrong door, she realized
She was too engrossed on the way to
cross-check
That she reached the wrong destination

Surprised, she wondered at the cause
How somehow a wrong turn landed her right
there
A missed left and wrong right
Some right paths, some wrong guides

Before she could leave, the door opened
Stood before her, her soulmate
One who held her close
One who was her destiny
In the wrong turns, she found the right one
Grateful she gave up all scrutiny

A lasting love

A fleeting moment
The first look
The first touch
The last hug
The first pain
Ever so precious
Never too late
Fight with it
Fight for it
Fleeing love
Throbbing pain
Cherished memories
Time a fleeting
Truly giving
Never expecting
Enchanted life
Blissful existence

The Fort

She decided to let go
Of the love that never reciprocated
Of the care that never came back
Of the hope that never realized
Of the pain that throbbed her heart
Of the loss that pinched her soul
Of the grief that was inflicted so heartlessly

She instead decided to
Be the love that she wanted
Care for herself
Realize her own hopes
Soothe her own heart
Protect her own soul
Be happy in her own ways

A magic happened when she took back control
The world around did not matter anymore
She built around her a fort
That no one could now conquer
The bricks to her fort were the hurts they inflicted
Their ruthlessness was the cement
She took the pieces of her broken heart
And made a palace out of her ruins

Today as she rises, the world is in awe
Their plans to break her down, futile
As they see her scale new heights and wonder
What was the Woman made of

Rediscovered

A golden path unintendedly
Led her to a trench of thorns
Her rose-tinted glasses
Couldn't see the upcoming danger
She went ahead with a full heart
Which got hurt by them instead
For that, what she considered her glory
Came a slurry of hatred instead

Friends lost, foes gained
Her pain knew no limits
Alone and forlorn
Bleeding, her heart felt a churn
Her intellect her enemy,
Leading to a spiral of overthinking
About the outcome and the world
She soon lost her sense of self

The porosity of her mind
Was what led her out, though
For within the hell of her soul
She discovered a new version of herself
Her strength rekindled slowly
Brimming with grace
No amount of hatred
Could touch the beauty of her days
She didn't know her true power
She thought she was a delicate flower
But within her soul
Lied a power to behold
Rediscovered truly
Even if now on her own

Hopes

Like the first ray of sunshine
Brightening the darkness away
Hope crept into her grief-laden heart
Filing it up slowly and gently

At first she resisted, clouds of doubt too
strong to go away
Then surrender started slowly coming; life
energies now aligned
For now, they found a plan
a plan made of chaos
She quietly surrendered
finding a torch within her own

There was a beauty in the hope of her heart
The melody of her heartbeat, too strong
She didn't need anyone to believe in her
anymore
Her hope, enough to float her along
Her passion, a fire, too strong in her now
She didn't need anyone no more,
Her heart, now empty of desire
The light of life was too strong to be dimmed
With a few comments or disbeliefs
She was here to serve
Feel the happiness she deserved and
Walk away from those who didn't belong

Fairy Tales

She recalled her childhood
Filled with tales of possibilities
Of coming back from the dead
Of finding love in tragedy

She stood facing her reality
Where truth took away her dreams
Love lost despite giving it all
And dying each day till actually
Passion and truthfulness ignored
Being cheated on by her own

Hoping and faith felt like such a childish
dream
She felt afraid, though no more
As the dream though broken
Made way for a new path
The truth about it, harsh
but it was freeing at last

Now in reality she takes a flight
Love and life were not a gift from others
But a boon she was born with
No more waiting, but only creating
She now lived to make her own tale

Too Much

He said she was too much
She loved too much
She spoke too much
She messaged too much
She cared too much
She cried too much
She hugged him too much
She wanted him too much
So, he fell for her too much

After a while, he couldn't handle her
brightness
His interest in her soon began to digress
She was too opinionated

She was too loud
She was too outspoken
She was too proud
He criticized her passion
He criticized her ambition
He criticized her voice
He criticized her tone
He picked up his cell phone and
Told her to leave him alone
She did not cry and walked away in an instant
The light in her heart was her only constant
She knew she was too much
And will always be too much
She will fight for her true self too much
She will protect her light too much
Now she may be alone while she continues to
be too much
Her heart is positive that she will find true
love, even if she has to wait, too much

The Last Call

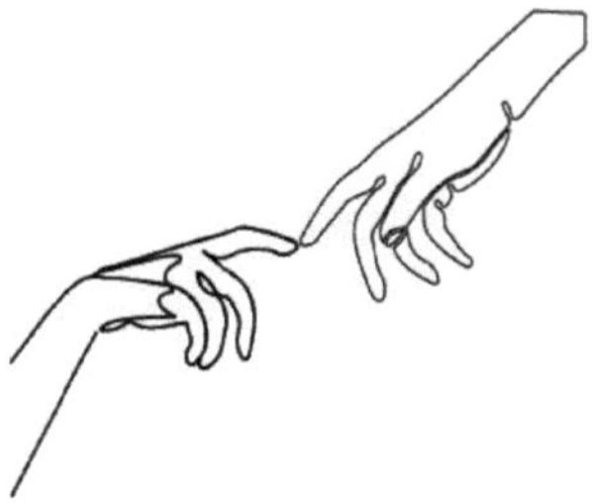

For some, it was just another day
But she was worried
She was breathless
She was exhilarated, so much, that her nerves
twitched endlessly
She had a call coming in and she was worried
That her voice would give away
that she still loved him
That her silence may give away
that she still believed that he was the one for
her
That her eyes may give away
that she was still waiting for him
That the goodbyes may give away
that she believed that he was always within
her

Despite the pain
The distance
The misunderstandings
Her heart still belonged to him
And maybe he would never reveal his cards
She knew he loved her silently
As his actions and inactions
His care, his affection
His sacrifice, his heart
Was not unseen by her
Even if he will never reveal his heart ever
She knew that his love was true

Better than yesterday

Under the guise of love
Comes pain, chasing her heart
Slowly unfolding
Greatly overbearing

Like a shadow in the dark
It crept away, leaving a mark
Her body broken
Her soul depleted
Her mind fleeting
Hope eroded with disdain

Losing him was her biggest fear
He claimed that he will always be near
He said so without committing
He later took off anyways

She was no predator
But he claimed to be the prey
He left her heartbroken
And full of despair

She took a path untrodden
She would not allow to be broken
She would be better than yesterday
each and every day
She would in herself find her true love
One who would hold up promises
One who would really care
And the only one with whom she would really
share

Dis ease

Scrambling in her bed
Not ready to wake up
The job, which was a dream
Was now a nightmare

Her heart not at ease
Voices screamed a distant note
Her heartbeat was fast
The clock a ticking
Proving, running, and achieving
Things which were at her fingertips
Now seemed difficult
Smallest of worries into great issues
Her mind triggered at the shortest concerns
Dis eased and dis heartened

Prodigy once-in-a-lifetime mind
Decided to lead the race

She was a human in the race surrounded by rats
Scrambling and biting each other to pieces
Hell she wanted to win
But she lost herself in exchange
Till she realized that she lost so much
That she finally lost it
She was dying inside
Her body just running in vain

A mystical sound called her
It was her own heartbeat
That called her to live, just live
As long as she was alive, everything would work out
Yes it will, it will
Shunning the world
She shut herself down
Looking in deep
Finding her true retreat
She knew what she wanted
She did what she wanted
And freed her heart
No longer dis eased now
she spreads love and is alive

To be loved

To be loved is to be hopeful
To be loved is to be respected and be
respectful
To be loved is to sometimes be hurt
To be loved is to be cared for silently

It makes no noise; it needs no awards
Its biggest reward is the look in your eyes
The knowing look that it is your home
The soothing look that it is your prize
The lustful look that it is your pleasure
The look of compassion that it is the one,
whose pain you care for
The look of kindness that empathizes with its
pain
The look of gratitude for all that it gives

A true love

A love that is silent, less words, more action
Listening to the heartbeat, that is all the
medicine you need
A love that is resilient,
always steady and strong
A love is that is sometimes misguided,
not knowing how to express what it feels
Words not matching its thoughts at times
and it doesn't know how to heal

Don't expect it to express; don't expect it to
heal you
Don't expect it to know nor expect it to feel
you
Or Your heart will break
and expectations will crumble
You need to remember, true love is only

action
You need to remember, true love needs no
verbal expression
You need to remember, true love will hurt
you at times
You need to remember, that you gave it this
right

For all the heartbreak, all the pain,
all the longing and all the suffering,
True love is worth it
As it stands true to the test of time

The tigress lies in the bed alone

She lies in the bed alone, ordering the grocery
She lies in the bed alone, planning, while her kids think her a mockery
She lies in the bed alone, making to-do lists
She lies in the bed alone, ordering unreasonably expensive gifts
She lies in the bed alone, thinking the kid needs a new file
She lies in the bed alone, fussing about the laundry pile

She lies in the bed alone, scrolling mindlessly
She lies in the bed alone, biting her nails carelessly
She lies in the bed alone, with no time for

skincare
She lies in the bed alone, looking for the cheapest airfare
She lies in the bed alone, fussing over a torn cuticle
She lies in the bed alone, wondering why she doesn't look beautiful
She lies in the bed alone, thinking it's been a while
She lies in the bed alone, hoping and wanting to reconcile
She lies in the bed alone, with her mind fluttering with memories of the past
She lies in the bed alone, thinking this was supposed to last

She lies in the bed alone, wishing it could be mended
She lies in the bed alone, thinking her world has ended

She lies in the bed alone, now making her bucket list
She lies in the bed alone, and she plans to conquer Everest

She lies in the bed alone, reading Jane Austen
She lies in the bed alone, planning a solo trip
to Boston
She lies in the bed alone, setting up an early
alarm
She lies in the bed alone, fondling her newly
bought charm
She lies in the bed alone, finding solace in her
solitude
As now her soul has reached a different
altitude
She chooses each day to alter her attitude
toward her loneliness
And now the world finally knows that she is
truly a Tigress

Goddess

Everyone wanted something from her
Her love
Her care
Her wisdom
Her freedom
Her passion
Her ambition
She quietly gave it to them

No one gave her what she wanted
Their love
Their care
Their kind words
Their appreciation

She didn't know who she was

And was soon depleted
The world saw her fade away
Like the sunset, her light now dim
Till one day the inner eye reminded her
that she was a never-ending ocean
With time, she realized she was love
She realized she was life
She realized the power of her solitude
She felt a new stride of life

Her face started glowing
Her smile returned
Her aura cleared
it had found itself

She was a goddess
Who needed nothing and no one
Other than her third eye
That opened within her
To unravel the life she really was
The power that lay within her
Of beauty
Of love
Of spirit
Of life

Sunset on a Dune

Watching the sun set sitting on a sand dune
She felt so alone in the crowd that
surrounded her
Taking selfies, making poses
They were all too busy to see the beautiful
synchronicity of the sun, earth, life, and
existence
The magnanimity of it all
The enormity of it all

The screaming kids
The expecting spouses
The people scrambling for the best sunset
shots
All of that felt like a world away
As just for a moment, her mind expanded
She realized what a miracle to be alive

She felt a grain of sand in her hand and felt so small in its comparison
The world was enormous
and she didn't know anything at all
The beauty of being small,
the magic of being still,
the power of being a no one
gave her a sense of peace within

Tomorrow she would return to the world
But at this moment she felt at complete peace
She would be mother, boss, woman tomorrow
Today just for a few moments, she would be it all
Yet nothing at all at the same time
Just a few moments to herself
Just a few moments being herself

Unafraid

She was trapped in the wrong place
They thought she would die
But she was a crazy woman who kept smiling
As if nothing had happened
It was surprising how light she felt after she
started saying no
It was amazingly freeing and beautifully
liberating though
How will she manage the expenses, who will
take care of the mortgage
was a question she did not care for an answer

She was settling for less and she was done
So she packed her briefcase and said she will have no more
She wanted to fly and they wanted to clip her wings
She will not have it; she will not stop living
She will not be unkind
She will not do something that is not her
She will not appease anyone
She walked away with her head held high
She will not bow down in front of anyone but God

Nothingness

People told her she was just like her father
Little did she know they said so mockingly
People told her she was just like her mother
Little did she know they said so with disdain

As she grew up, she realized she was
unwanted and had no one
But this meant she was free to find her own
path and be her own sun
As she walked the streets barefoot, she smiled
She didn't know she was missing anything
and she wanted nothing
Her nothingness was her bliss

Somehow the food appeared
She took shelter under the trees
She stared in awe at the starry skies at night
Living her life independently with no possessions
She shared, she cared, and she dared
She had no degree and the streets were her home
She had no glory nor any epic story
She was complete in her nothingness

Miss Delulu

She found courage to fulfil her dreams
Dreams that had long been stifled by screams

She found courage to go out alone
She didn't give a damn to the criticism to
which she would be prone

She found courage to laugh out loud
She didn't care about those too proud

She found courage to stand up for her kids so
they wouldn't be bound
They wouldn't go through what she had to,
not as long as she was around

She found courage to be her true self, wild
and free
For she was one of a kind of a woman, too
bad they couldn't see

She found courage amongst the cruel words
of others
For now she was a free soul, unconcerned and
not bothered

She found courage to accept her true
feminine energy
Wild but caring, spirited and free, together
with her lover, they created synergy

They said she was delusional
to ignore her fear but she found courage
amidst the harshness of the world
Her lover could have found solace in her
strong bosom,
but he left Miss Delulu alone
Miss Delulu, true to her name, did not care
For a man who couldn't recognize her true
strength was not worthy of her

Blue Lotus

She became quiet
No words left to say
She became restless
She became restrained

Only if she cared any longer
Only if it really mattered
Like a Blue Lotus, beautiful and rare
Her insides rose above the dirt around
Beautiful and pure
Unharmed by her exterior

She was like a blue lotus
Born again
Growing again
Growing toward her freedom
Growing toward her true self
Growing with love
Becoming love
The growth of her heart
Taking her miles apart

More than her son

She taught the girl how to talk and walk
How best the food is to be cooked
She loved the girl more than her own son
She taught her to be independent

She taught the girl how to be observant and keen
And attend to others' needs
She loved the girl more than her own son
She taught her to be caring

She taught the girl how to serve and smile
And be the polite hostess
She loved the girl more than her own son
She taught her to be pleasant

She taught the girl how to take care of her
family
And not give weight to her egos
She loved the girl more than her own son
She taught her to be a giver

She reminded the girl that she may be a
Leader at her work
But at home, she was a provider
She loved the girl more than her own son
She taught her to be humble

She taught the girl how to take care of kids
And manage her job together
She loved the girl more than her own son
She taught her to be a working mother

The necessary GoodBye

The heart was deprived
The soul now barren
Replaced and eluded
Ignored and rejected

Feigning ignorance
Doesn't excuse the hurt caused
Running away,
Does not mean the love now paused
Some goodbyes were necessary
Even if her heart bled
Holding her broken pieces
away she was led

Unaware and blissful
Her caretaker slept
While she lay all broken
With rowdy, unkempt hair all over her bed
Searching for love left her empty
Freeing her soul was her pain
Some goodbyes were necessary
As toward her freedom, they now led

Something within her changed
As hope walked out of the door
There she stood wounded, unable to sleep
She thought her life was meant to go deep
Next day she found her love in her favorite meal
Love in her outfit
Love in her song
Never invasive, always beautiful
slowly but surely beginning to heal
Life's tragedies make the greatest warriors
On the battlefield of life, she would be soon ready to roar

She always said I love You

He never said I Love You, and he never shared
He never said I Love You, but he cared
He never said I Love You, but was kind
He never said I Love You, and he did not let
her know what was on his mind
He never said I Love You, and he made her
wait quite a while
He never said I Love You, but he made her
smile

She loved him and thought they would always be together
She was horribly mistaken, and they never got their forever
One fine day, she woke up and poof he was gone
Just a message left at early dawn
She was left alone to mend her broken heart
She tried to fight him back, but he tore her hope apart
He knew he left her for her own good
She deserved better and he knew where he stood

Little did he know he tore away the last shred of hope in her heart
He didn't see himself the way she saw him: full of light, love, and smart
Her days blackened, her eyes swollen, she struggled to tell the day from night
Even a slight glimpse of him made her chest go tight

With time she accepted that he would never feel the way she felt

Maybe he would never be with her and now
nor did she expect
Days turned to months, and she slowly
started to heal
Her broken heart had now again begun to feel
She knew she would never have him, but it
didn't matter anymore
She was love and life personified and so much
more

He never said I Love You, and he broke her
heart
He never said I Love you and went away miles
apart
Her love for him was not dependent on
having any gain
She always said I Love You, and she would go
through the pain again.

Never Alone

A string that held the hearts
Beating violently but rhythmically together
She thought about him
With every breath
Every song, every hurt
Every promise, every word

His love found her sinking heart
And mended it with his smile
It was her illusion
And a cry for the love that she deserved
In those fleeting moments, she lived for a lifetime
He assured her she would never be alone
She believed him and now
Even abandoned by him she is whole

His absence made her heart stronger
But her soul, emptier
She learned to be alone
She learned to be alright

The one

You need to find the one
The one that will make you whole
You need to find the one
The one that will give you it all
You need to find the one
The one that will share your pain
You need to find the one
The one that will make you feel
You need to find the one
The one that will be there for you
You need to find the one
The one that will give you joy
You need to find the one
The one that will give you meaning

So she searched for the one
In her parent, partner, and child
But none of them gave her anything
Taking everything away instead
Feeling empty and broken
She lay wondering where could she find the one
Closing her eyes she let out a sigh
she found the one under her own eyes
She was looking for the one
The one to hold
The one to cherish
The one to love
The one to be
The one that was always hidden inside her
Finally unfolding her heart, she found her lover

The Choice

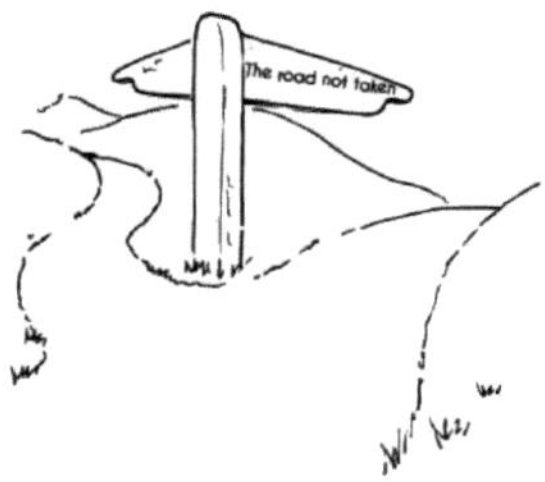

She chose to be silent
She chose to be in pain
She chose to be resilient
She chose to be responsible
She chose to love unconditionally
She chose to cry inconsolably
She chose to forgive
She chose to forget

She chose a path untrodden
She chose to be fine with being broken
She chose to not be a princess
She chose to be a warrior
In her heartbreak, she found her peace
In her pain, she found her strength
She chose to be herself
She chose life

Realizations

The piercing eyes brimming with hatred
The sharp words hurting her pride
The critical look
The stigma attached
She was just a child who didn't know her
power
Till she was condemned to be the swan in a
family of crows

Her beauty, her brains,
her power, her fame
They condemned her for being different
They condemned her for being brilliant
She was just a child who didn't know her
stature
Till she was condemned to be the swan in a
family of crows

Her love, her care,
her virtues, her flair
They condemned her for being loving
They condemned her for her care
She was just a child who didn't know her sweetness
Till she was condemned to be the swan in a family of crows

Her strength, her determination,
her focus, her ambition
They condemned her for being hopeful
They condemned her for her vision
She was just a child who didn't know her capabilities
Till she was condemned to be the swan in a family of crows

Her sympathy, her kindness
her caring heart, her gentleness
They condemned her for being loving
They condemned her for her care
She was just a child who didn't know forgiveness
Till she was condemned to be the swan in a family of crows

The sun of their existence

He was the sun of their existence
their world revolved around him
Like the maestro, he took all the decisions
His glory and pride holding it all

He was looking for someone to bring within
his orbit
She seemed to be the pretty homely one
So he charmed her, hiding away his worst
She was keen to feel his warmth
So she agreed at first
but little had she anticipated
Like Icarus, her wings would be burnt for life
For that world she moved to, revolved around
him
While she was forced to be bound

Years passed by and she forgot she could fly
Till she met her twin
One stolen glance and she was hooked
She moved again; it was time to fly
It was good for a moment but she was burnt again soon
This time for good
She spent her last years alone in peace at having tried
It was clear she was born to fly
Even if just for a minute
That minute was enough to give her a lifetime of happiness
She had waited now for long
so she flew and burnt her wings away
and told the world "So long!"

The Rare Diamond

She went to the best parties
She wore the best clothes
She had the latest accessories
She was the envy of the town
But sleeping on a king-size bed
she felt alone every night

She had meals that were only light
She had to always look right
For the trophy she chose to be
She thought she was the talk of the town
The glamour of her looks would vanish one
day without a sound

He was tired of her demands
He was tired of taking her around
He wanted to be loved back
This time around
She cared more about how she looked
She was busily clicking away everything good
She catered to his body but not to his soul
She wanted validation to feel whole

Tired frustrated
He wanted to be free but was bound by duty
But one fine day he had enough, so he set himself free
It wasn't honorable, but he finally didn't care
Virtue was optional
Freedom was final
She lost a diamond that was the rarest of all
Just to prove to the world that she had it all

The Lost Boy

His mind seemed always in a fight mode
His aura made people stare
His words like piercing arrows
Always ripped the target bare
His passion, beyond control
His reputation preceded him
They ran away like a flock on fire
As soon as they heard him come

He craved attention
so he always created a sound
Even if that made others bleed
Not that it was his intention
One day he retired and soon enough
The attention slowly receded
It was the position that had the glory
It was the name that had the fame

He sulked and screamed
He shouted and threw a fit
He behaved like a toddler
Who just lost his candy
His loved ones kept their patience
But his ego didn't concede
He was someone and thereby
He didn't need to recede

His death came suddenly
And his people were relieved quietly
Small, insignificant, he was now just dust
No one remembered his glory
All rejoiced to be finally free of his fits
No one will remember his story

Blanky

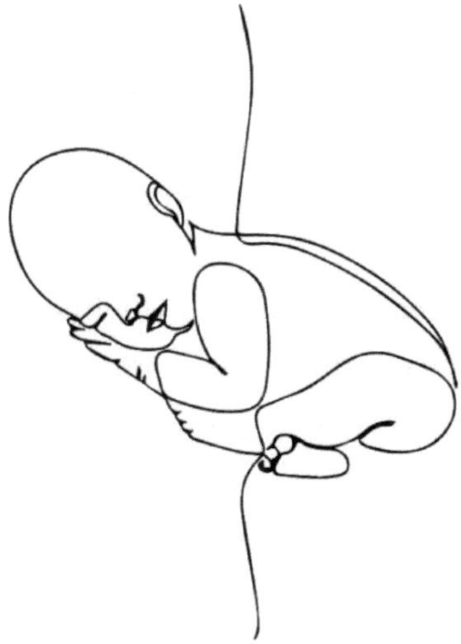

The little one had a comfy blanky
One that he didn't want to leave
But it was time for school; the blanky
wouldn't look cool
So he left the blanky back home
At school, he kept thinking about his blanket
As he missed its cozy feeling
So he looked for familiar faces around
In search of the missed warmth, alas to be
disappointed

With each passing day, the blanky was now worn out
Its warmth didn't last very long
It didn't fit quite well now
And his fingers were very sore
Trying to pull away at corners

Times wasted and hours now whiled away
Finding the comfort in its company
This blanky was never going to fit
No matter how hard he tried
Tired now, he gave up trying to fit in
Stepping outside, he felt finally relieved
The blanky, now too small to reach it
Outside the blanky, he grew tall fast
Within it, his growth was stunted
Growth that for which he was born

The True Winner

He couldn't give her money
He didn't have fame
He just owned a true heart
One that knew no game

She understood him, loved him beyond expectation
She was everything he wanted
With him, she had no fears
His smile, the cure for her tears
For him, she would take up all the pain

She was a tornado for the world but
For him, she wanted to be the gentle rain
Together they felt understood and seen like never before

So beautifully were they bound
She fought with him
She fought for him
He had never experienced love so gentle but
strong
That he now feared his dream may not last
long
He loved her so he wanted to set her free
She needed to get away to prosper
He thought he would never be able to give
her anything
Not the happiness she deserved
So he asked her to leave again and again
Till she agreed
How could she say no to her soulmate
Even if that would make her bleed

She understood his heart and never asked for
more
She was the twin of his beautiful soul
She wished he could see that her love was
pure
That he deserved so much more
Only if he knew who he was truly deserved
Not all love is measured in gold

Away now but closer than ever before
His heart was only for her
She loves him despite odds
No distance can affect her heart
Even tomorrow she will always be his
Her heart needed no more bliss
He won the game of life and love
Through his gentle sacrifice
Her love, her heart, it is still his now
The true winner emerged by taking the fall

Savior

He was not her savior, nor did she need one
Love, commitment, and time she wanted none
She was a strong woman who just needed a man in front of whom she could crumble
His presence was enough; he was enough to make her fumble

She opened up her heart to him, shared her vulnerabilities
She went on and on but never shared her capabilities
He left her as he felt he was not ready to be her savior

Little did he know she didn't need one, nor
needed any favor
She trusted him with her deepest secrets
Their love was supposed to be deep knit
But that scared him with expectations that
came along
He thought she deserved someone more
strong

She didn't realize, he would be so heartless
To leave a woman who would have left the
world for him regardless
She broke down when he left, staying up all
night
Their love was too important to let go
without a fight
She let go of her pride and tried again and
again
Till he made it clear there was nothing left
between them then
It was not him that she missed, it was how she
felt while with him

With him, she could be an unfiltered naughty
child; with him, she felt joyful to the brim

So, she made herself all that and more but
this time without him
His memories slowly faded away and he no
longer an extended limb
With this, she fixed her torn-up heart
Piece by piece glued together, never to be
broken apart

A heart that started beating again when she
met him
A heart that now no longer misses him
A heart that now healed will always be
thankful for him
Even though he left it all on a whim

Destroyer of love

He knew her love would destroy everything,
including his ego
He knew her love would destroy it all
But for once he didn't care
And was ready to take the fall

He knew she would give up everything for
him
Her family, her life, and her kids
He tried but could not do the same
He was supposed to be a man of honor
So he broke her heart and left her alone
She resisted as she knew his love
His love was no obligation
He deserved to be loved back
By a woman who loved him with her soul

But for his sake, she agreed to be apart
So they could fulfill their obligations
Away in the eyes of the world
But can true love ever be apart?

Husband

His love was fiercely protective and strong at first
Filling her heart with hope
His love was sometimes gently possessive
Filling her heart with a sense of belonging
His love was sometimes a gentle guiding force
Filling her heart with a sense of direction
His love was sometimes proud
Filling her heart with a sense of achievement
His love was sometimes childish
Filling her heart with a need to pamper

His love was sometimes protective
Filling her heart with a sense of being cared for
His love was sometimes overbearing
Filling her heart with a need to stand up for itself
His love was sometimes nurturing
Filling her heart with a sense of being loved despite her vulnerabilities
His love was ever evolving, and it changed its shades every day
His love is sometimes hidden and sometimes out there
His love is impactful, leaving a mark on her heart and soul
Love of good man was her biggest blessing
His name imprinted on her body, mind, and soul forever
Her husband, her forever

Dedicated to my loving Husband

Tears

Tears lost their meaning
As they flowed every instant
Gently caressing his face
Slowly smudging into a blot
Reminding him of the love he lost
Reminding him of the love he let go

She had now closed her heart
She no more shared anything with him
Merely existing as a name
in his contact list
Was a love that could have been
Was a friendship that could have been
Was a connection now severed
A soulmate that could have seen

Tears unstoppable
Fears now real
She was gone
He pushed her too hard
She was gone
He pushed her too real

She would come back
If he really tried
But his tears blinded him
Fear crept over his sight
Love isn't a deal to be lost
All she needed from him was an attempt
Only if his tears hadn't blinded him
Only if he wasn't afraid of getting hurt again

Brave

Honorable and almighty
So-called virtuous man stands tall
Slashing his sword, winning mighty battles
Today he may fall
Today he may rise
His ego now gets a flare
He scorns the meek woman, who cooks his meal
He pushes away the beggar on the street
He laughs at the boy too weak to push a cart

Deep in the forest lives a man
With no hut and not a possession of his own
He walks a mile to feed his child
He works hours at a stretch without a complaint
Lovingly gives what is his

Hopes and Desires and all
Fulfilled, he sleeps at night
He needs no glory nor a gift
Waiting patiently, grateful for each day
As he braves the storm and the wind
To survive and do his due
Not intent to leave a mark
True bravery lying in the mundane love
One that needs no glory nor any fame

The wounded child

The child screamed
The child taunted
With words that hurt
Uttered without regret
Hurting others without excuse
Talking incessantly about his greatness
Keeping safe distance
The loved ones moved away

Kindness absent in his heart
Hurtful glances in his eyes
With time the child grew distant
No friends in sight
His wounds exposed
No words were then found

One day a kind soul
Nevertheless, gave it some notice
Loved him despite his harshness
Loved him despite the abuses
Slowly the wounds filled
The child grew fuller
His soul now saved
From his own misguided thoughts

The fallen angel

Slowly breathing his last
Lay down a creature
Self-righteous and all-consuming
Proud and arrogant
His family cared for him till the end
While living, his ego did never bend

After death, they chose to remember
All that was good
Shunned him they never
Nor loved him for what he stood

He chooses his ego
And they chose their love
Overshadowing his acts of evil
Seeing the purity of their soul
Stunned the world, did wonder
The courage they did gather
To overlook his heinous acts
To let go of all the trouble
It wasn't so difficult, you see
We keep with us what is precious
His acts reflected his incomplete soul
Allowing it to overcome them, never the goal

The purity of their soul was a gem
That could not be thrown away on a whim
His evil intentions could never be successful
As their souls never agreed to split
With his body, his acts left their home with
him
What remained was love and light that they
own

Conflict

How dare he not listen
How dare he use his mind
How dare he go against me
The arrogant father cried

The boy was now a man
The father's dictates now ignored
Fully grown with a mind of his own
He conveyed his wishes
The father simply got bored
And ordered him some more prizes

He knew he was born to fly
He knew his father was careful
But he wanted to try

His eyes all hopeful
His father didn't take it easy
His words were final
He didn't care about his plight
He gave this man his life

How dare he betray his creator
How dare he go against his word
He was just a puppet; he pulled the strings
What he said mattered
The man retaliated and went over the edge
A fallen angel for sure
Entrenched himself in his passion, he fled
An addiction with no cure
The conflict of his soul
The hunger for power
The need to control
Made him forget the love they once held

Losing his son was his biggest defeat
He refused to be his trophy
No one could now stop his feet
He won, and his life now rosy?

The disciple

The disciple woke up early every day
The disciple regularly slept
The disciple had a rigid schedule
Of lists and glory, all kept
He followed each checklist recommended
Of things to do and that not
Leaving all his soul's insights away
As they didn't adhere to the world's say

The disciple grew weary of the mundane
His soul dying each day
In search of life, maybe even a wife
The disciple ran away
He chose to be the disciple of life now
Living truly with joy each day
Breaking norms
Living life
Not caring about fitting in
True lover of life and play

Service

He expected love unconditional
Servitude with compassion
He was a gentle soul who loved
And gave without complaints
But he never found a love like himself
Breaking his heart in two
He gave up his desires
For his loved ones
Serving, being there always
But at the slightest discomfort
they pushed back vehemently
Forgetting all his love and comfort

Pain eluded all the happiness
A single thorn piercing his heart
As long as he was of service, they cared
His unconditional love, now for granted
His being was strong
Love needs to move on
His soul needed protection
From the ungratefulness around

Strength of character, more than chatter
Service and function, as we are men of action
He won't turn back now
His debt now over

Doubts of love

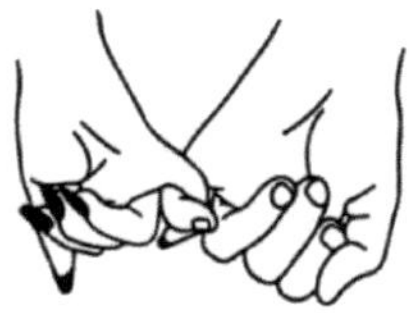

The risk too much
His pride on line
Clouds of doubt floating
Covering his sight
With sweaty palms and rapid breaths
He took himself to greater depths

The price of ambition
His loved one's faith
Clouds of doubt floating
Pushing him to a corner
With crumbling ambition and fear's blows
He took himself to greater lows

Though his fears realized
The love within always stood by his side
Clouds of doubt now disappearing
Life now becoming a flow
With a loving heart and a gentle soul
He walked toward a greater goal

New Life

The mother was bleeding incessantly
She was born in the night
The mother couldn't see anything else
Other than her tiny hands and beautiful eyes
She went through pain alone for hours
Her loved ones slept peacefully, deaf to her screams
Pain is normal they said, nothing but to bleed
The mother walked around briskly, thinking only about the child

She was left to navigate things alone
She was meant to deal with all the pain
That night the girl who cried over every little thing
went through the greatest pain alone
a mother was born with each stride
Holding on to hope of a new life

That night she learned resilience
That night she became one with the universe
At that moment she was too blinded by the
pain
To realize the miracle that occurred
The life she knew ended that night
For with her daughter was born a mother

Barren

The heights and depths
The vastness and immensity
Of time
And space
And her body
All seemed like a blank canvas

Like a barren tree now spurting new life
She woke up to find silence in the noise
The music did not reach her ears
The silence consoled her fears
Today was a fix but tomorrow won't be sore

She didn't crave freedom anymore
She felt her spirit lifted
Love, life, and laughter spilled
And just like that
She was free from all guilt

Tomorrow didn't matter
Nor did any memories make her cry
She was a force of nature
All she knew was to fly

Her heart was whole again
Love within her the glue
The fear and worries now gone
Disappeared in thin air
She was courage personified
All she knew was to dare

Mind, heart, and soul
Together said to her
She was meant to leave a mark, wherever she went
She was glory reincarnated
All she knew was to succeed

Her love did come back
She felt his voice call her gently
And felt his firm heartbeat, as he filled her
with himself
She was the sweetness of honey
All she knew was to love

She was finally loved
The way she deserved to be
It was more than she imagined
And soon exploding her body
Came out her beautiful heart
Who she now calls her son

Her heart was full
Her soul was whole
She was life reimagined
All she knew was to live

A Mother's morsel

Her hands were sore from working
Her feet had done everything but rest
She came home to find me
Looking like a dirty mutt at best
She threw away her bag
Her warm arms held me tender
She hurried to get me cleaned
For her, I was a princess, and to me, she was
my Queen

After I was cleaned and fed
She remembered something and fled
Out came the laptop and she ticked away
Till again she heard me yelp
I had been away for too long
She needed to be with me
Then with her gentle nudge I stopped
And in her arms, I fell

She sang me a sweet lullaby
While her phone kept ringing
But she dare not stop her singing
As I was her lovely baby
Stomach now squirming and insides churning
She put a morsel in her hand
But back in the plate it fell
As now it was papa's turn to yell

She had too much to do to eat
But her strength was slowly slipping
She took a morsel again in her hand
but almost immediately it now again fell
Papa had come and held me tight while he
proceeded to watch the game
I revolted and she came running back
Dry like an empty well
No respite in sight

I was satisfied finally so she left me to play
But now she left to clean up
One thing after another and time slipped
away
The morsel of food now cold

In her hand it came but
I screamed again; it was time for the princess to sleep
Like a woman possessed, she ran with her arms holding me
It was almost like a game that she won each time,
Just reaching every unreasonable target
That the demands around her placed
Oh so crazily
Her three full-time jobs
Now mixing up hazily

Her fingers almost twitched with victory, as she tried to put me to bed
But behold the next second, she fell off to sleep with me
Her heart was full but her body now drifted hungry, tired, and broken
The morsel of food still lies around
while all around her people stood pleasured

They took away her son

Bring him back to me
She screamed at the closing door
Bring him back to me
She yelled at every passerby on the road
Bring him back to me
She pleaded the judge
Bring him back to me
She prayed every day, now heartbroken
Bring him back to me
She repeated to the universe with tears in her eyes
He came back one day
At the age of 16
He didn't recognize her

but she did definitely
She couldn't tell him who she was
Or the shame would take away her son again
She finally smiled after an eternity
as she handed him the vegetables he bought

Remove the glasses

Mom, I am scared
He cried, clutching her arms
The Batman is just too strong
He keeps flying at me and destroying his enemy
But the Joker gives me the creeps
His wicked smile and those teeth
It is too scary
It is too real

Remove the 3D glasses
Nudged the mother
Trust me, it's a distant dream
Look, it's the actors on the screen
The fear was just inside of you

Nothing you see and feel here is true
Mom then why are we even here
Said the boy, now trembling with fear
To get a thrill, sometimes a chill
We are just here to enjoy the show
Time, when up, we have to go

His fear subsided
His anxieties faded
Smile was back on his face
He cheered for Batman now to show the
Joker his place

That night she kissed him Good Night
And he recognized the worries on her face
He knew his dad would never come back
The pain in her eyes hidden by her voice
Just remove the glasses Mom, I am always
here
Life will not be fair
Let us not fill it with despair
We are here just to enjoy the show, he said

Stillness

Still unfolding but not seeking
Still feeling but not caring
Still unending but not getting closer
Feelings of timelessness
Rising and falling
Feelings of emptiness
Coming and going
Past and future
Still lying and not existing
Present moment
Simply breathing
Lovingly ending

Beautifully beginning
Soul singing a melody
Gently with harmony
Life reaching newer heights
Suddenly soaring
Ecstasy or blissfulness
Reached within a moment
Life felt in a moment
Stillness in her being

Self

The self was all-consuming
Bursting with pride and ego
He didn't care if people were lost
He didn't care if they didn't smile
He simply wanted obedience
Shouting orders out to them
He simply was in denial
Power and prestige, his fuel

Brimming with confidence for the world
But empty inside
Only if he had filed it with purpose
Instead of pride

Only if he had filled it with authenticity
Instead of fear
Only if he had filled it with care
Instead of desire
The self could have reached greater heights
But pity it now just lies

The God Particle

Away from the wild world
Lay a beauty at rest
She wasn't aware of who she was
And had to go through a test
She was not aware
It had been years
Her fears tested
Her tears rolled
She had forgotten to be happy
She had forgotten to be free
She had missed her life she thought
In this grief and moment

Her mind had become a puzzle
Her life, just a speck
Till she met the God particle
And off her life got calmer
She was like a photon particle
Constantly rushing around
Till she reached a velocity
That burst her soul
But out came a particle out of the hole
And suddenly her hand caught the same

Nothing compared to its shine, no money, no fame
In the particle, she found the freedom of her soul
In the particle, she found the whole console
The earth, the solar system, the galaxy, et al.
Within it, she found the deepest ocean
And secrets unfolded all of a sudden
Her heart knew she now needed no meaning
As in the God particle, she found that it was irrelevant
All she needed was to keep her eyes open
And be in awe of the miracle that she called life

The Artist

Like a blank canvas stood the world
The artist amused by the potential
It looked at it with love and wondered
What would make the greatest painting of all

So he splattered some paint and made the
universe
A dose of black for the cosmos
A splash of red for the stars and solar systems
But he wanted it to be lively
So he added a splash of greens and blues to
the earth
But the painting didn't speak to him yet, so
he decided to make life
Plants, animals, birds, et al.
But he thought, how would they know what
to do with life
He needed a thinking being
so he splashed the picture with intellect,
creating a human

But the man drove the nature of the painting
with its ambition
So he splattered love to make a woman, who
would add love and heart to it
Man learned to love and
Together they produced more life
The artist was satisfied and loved the painting
But then life started wanting more and more
Forcing the artist to keep going
Money, wealth and possessions grew

The artist was tired as humans knew no
appreciation
It kept asking for more and more
Tired, he decided to walk away
Never to be found easily again
He hid himself in a tiny corner within the
human's soul
Only to be found by those who care to see
inside

The Gardener

The gardener stands displeased
The earth of his garden needs too much work
Determined, he pulls out his tools and gets going
Hours at end, he kept toiling
Now it was time to spread the seeds of his love
Gently caressing the ground, he allows them to settle
Watering them with care and hope

Days passed before he saw some shoots spring up
Reflecting new hopes for life
But birds dropped by to pluck and pull

He lost his sleep keeping them away
Managed to keep a few alive; he continues with the toil
Each day working toward the garden of his life
Now the seedlings grow into plants capable of growing by themselves
At last, I can rest, the Gardener said
Finally, some respite

He dozed off for what felt like a second
But an unruly garden welcomed him back
Oh, what a mess!
He pulled out his shears; it was now time to prune
He kept going on and on till June
The rain then nurtured his garden further
His load slowly started getting softer
With time, his body felt at ease
The gardener stood proud watching his garden
Never wanting to leave
The sights, the smells, it all enticed him

Then one day he was forced to leave

And into the earth he fell
At heaven's door, he cried for his garden
pleading to his God
Wondering who will look after it
I made it all; without me, it would fall
I really need to be back, he started to call

God smiled and said— you made it indeed
Let me show you what it looks like without
you
The garden he created looked even more
radiant,
with more flowers, bees, and birds around
So much beauty, so much sound
Shocked stood the gardener, wondering who
replaced him
when a light shone around him and he
understood
The cosmos provides and we are mere tools
Life goes on without him
The garden merely came through him
It never belonged to him
the true gardener was still around
there tending to the garden of life,
safe and sound

The Critic

Like a demon breaking its disguise
The critic raises its ugly head
Nothing and no one is good enough
No truth, no word, no rhyme
It creeps in slowly, understated
Quashing dreams and pulling plugs
Through doubt and fear
The world it does judge,
Merit notwithstanding

Tamed, it was a good servant
Running free, it's a murderer
Of dreams, of spirits
Of the fire that fuels dreams
Keeping the world in check
For it dares to dream a dream
For it should stay in check
Aspirations can kill
Befriended the critic, though works wonders
It doesn't deserve to rule
The world needs dreamers to take it far
Questioning its very core

What next

She saw a flower
So she started painting one
As she just finished the stem
She felt the sun looked better
So she decided to get the sun made first
But just as she splattered the yellow over the canvas
It spilled, covering the stem

Overwhelmed, she got a mop
And soon the canvas all blue
With red, she made some flowers
Dots of color all over
Smudging texture all around
With a sponge and a brush
Satisfied and urge completed
She left it to dry
The canvas was a mess
Could make out every naked eye

She held it in her hand, for every passerby to see
Most of them passed away, without a second glance
She held her head up loud and proud
Though wondering when she will get a real chance
She did this every day
Till people started to notice

A gentle lady thought she should open her eyes
The girl was wasting her life, in this distress
My dear—You are a miss; you shouldn't let

your hands stain
You are smart and pretty, she said
While these are good now, you should now
think what next to do
Let me clean your hands so

She smiled and hugged the lady tight
She was at ease now; someone was looking at
her plight
and not simply passing by as if to catch a
flight
Raised alone without anyone to love
Everyone around was so busy
Too busy to even catch a smile
She wanted just to make someone stop
And think about someone else
All around were just thinking about
themselves
What next, what next

Smiles

A flutter in the heart
Of words unspoken
A smile tying hearts together
A silent acceptance

A difficult moment
With lives changed
A smile healing the hurt heart
A silent consolation

A fear realised
With dreams now shattered
A smile promising the broken heart
A silent faith restoration

A new journey
With anticipation but excitement
A smile calming the anxious heart
A silent courage building

Memories

The heart's true treasure
Memories stand true to the test of time
Memories of love, slowly cherished
Memories of hate, truly perished
Memories of pain, truly hurting
Memories of gain, slowly fleeting

Memories, sometimes the only hope
Of times well lived
Of truly being loved
Memories sometimes truly drag him down
Of all the times failed
Of all the opportunities bailed

If only he could be wiped clean
Well won't life then be a dream
As for memories that haunt and make life
perish
A single memory notwithstanding, can make
faith cherish

Grace

Amidst the flowing river of life
There stood a lonely soul
Its path forgotten
Running around in circles
Walking but getting nowhere
Talking but getting nothing done

It stood exasperated, looking around
But true happiness was not found
Till it tore away the pretense
That what it held, was for it to own
Grace then found its path to its heart
True happiness was then found
Within the grace of its life's energy
Its world now found a new synergy
Things started falling into place
A pinch of faith kept the dream afloat

Tirelessly working, the soul now goes
But nothing feels like a burden anymore
For with grace and love, the path of thorns
now replaced
Lay ahead now a path paved toward his
growth